THE OFFICIAL
SUNDERLAND
ANNUAL 2020

WRITTEN BY
ROB AND BARBARA MASON
DESIGNED BY GEMMA MARTIN MIDDIS

A Grange Publication

© 2019. Published by Grange Communications
Ltd., Edinburgh, under licence from
Sunderland A.F.C. Printed in the EU.

Photographs © Getty Images / PA Images /
Ian Horrocks / Sunderland AFC / Barbara Mason /
Alan Hewson

ISBN 978-1-913034-31-3

CONTENTS

20 20 VISION

SECOND HALF OF THE SEASON

JANUARY

Home games with Lincoln, Wycombe and Doncaster get 2020 going, although if either Sunderland or Lincoln are in the third round of the FA Cup, the visit of the Imps will need re-arranging. January also sees The Lads travel to Fleetwood, Milton Keynes and Tranmere.

FEBRUARY

Any end of the January transfer window business Sunderland may want to do won't be helped by the first day of February bringing a long trip to Portsmouth. Coming after a midweek trip to Tranmere, it will be a busy time before a double-header at home to Ipswich and Rochdale. The month ends with journeys to Oxford and Coventry at either side of welcoming Bristol Rovers to Wearside.

MARCH

When the fixtures were published in the summer, March was a straightforward month with Saturday games at home to Gillingham, and trips to Blackpool and Southend. If games have been postponed because of international matches or involvement in the FA Cup, there's a good chance those fixtures will also take place this month. See safc.com/fixtures for up to date fixtures.

APRIL

Shrewsbury start the month at the Stadium of Light before Easter games at AFC Wimbledon on Good Friday followed by Peterborough at home on Easter Monday. There is then a trip to Burton who are likely to be promotion candidates before the final home game against Accrington Stanley.

MAY

Rotherham away on May 3rd is meant to be the last game of the season and hopefully it will be with Sunderland achieving automatic promotion. If Sunderland are in the play-offs again there will be more games to come. Rotherham was the venue for the last match of the season the previous time Sunderland were promoted from this level and everyone is hoping history repeats itself.

THREE TO THRILL

3

BOXING DAY BOLTON
SUNDERLAND V
BOLTON WANDERERS

Stadium of Light, Thursday 26 December 2019

Last season, Sunderland set a League One record attendance of 46,039 for the Boxing Day visit of Bradford City. This year the day after Christmas sees Bolton Wanderers come to the Stadium of Light. Relegated from the Championship last season, Bolton are a club who in the past have had a lot of success. Four times winners of the FA Cup, Bolton are grand opponents for what is traditionally a big day at the Stadium of Light.

TRACTOR BOYS
SUNDERLAND V
IPSWICH TOWN

Stadium of Light, Saturday 8 February 2020

Like Sunderland, Ipswich Town are used to playing at a higher level. The Tractor Boys crashed into League One last season and the men from Portman Road will be looking to bounce straight back so this could be a promotion showdown. England's two most successful managers are Sir Alf Ramsey and Sir Bobby Robson. Both of them became England boss and went on to become knights due to the success they created at Ipswich who became league champions under Ramsey and FA Cup and UEFA Cup winners under Robson.

DO THE STANLEY
SUNDERLAND V
ACCRINGTON STANLEY

Stadium of Light, Saturday 25 April 2020

The final home League One game of the season brings Accrington Stanley to Sunderland. They can be tricky opponents. With the lowest average crowd in League One last season – a modest 2,764 – Sunderland's average crowd last season of 32,157 meant that Accrington's total attendances for the entire season were fewer than two average gates at the Stadium of Light. That counts for nothing if Sunderland can't get the better of them and last year Stanley earned a 2-2 draw on Wearside. They will be determined to rise to the occasion again but at this stage of the season, Sunderland are unlikely to be able to drop points. Make sure you are there to help by cheering The Lads on!

2019-20 FIXTURES

DECEMBER

Thu 26 Dec	**Bolton Wanderers**	**H**
Sun 29 Dec	Doncaster Rovers	A

JANUARY

Wed 1 Jan	Fleetwood Town	A
Sat 4 Jan	**Lincoln City**	**H**
Sat 11 Jan	**Wycombe Wanderers**	**H**
Sat 18 Jan	MK Dons	A
Sat 25 Jan	**Doncaster Rovers**	**H**
Tue 28 Jan	Tranmere Rovers	A

FEBRUARY

Sat 1 Feb	Portsmouth	A
Sat 8 Feb	**Ipswich Town**	**H**
Tue 11 Feb	**Rochdale**	**H**
Sat 15 Feb	Oxford United	A
Sat 22 Feb	**Bristol Rovers**	**H**
Sat 29 Feb	Coventry City	A

MARCH

Sat 7 Mar	**Gillingham**	**H**
Sat 14 Mar	Blackpool	A
Sat 28 Mar	Southend United	A

APRIL

Sat 4 Apr	**Shrewsbury Town**	**H**
Fri 10 Apr	AFC Wimbledon	A
Mon 13 Apr	**Peterborough United**	**H**
Sat 18 Apr	Burton Albion	A
Sat 25 Apr	**Accrington Stanley**	**H**

MAY

Sun 3 May	Rotherham United	A

* Fixtures subject to change.

NEW BOYS

LEE
BURGE
GOALKEEPER

DATE SIGNED: 3ʳᵈ JULY 2019
LAST CLUB: COVENTRY CITY
ᴇʀ **CLUBS:** NUNEATON TOWN (LOAN)
ᴇʀNATIONAL: **ENGLAND UNDER 19**
AGE AT CHRISTMAS 2019: 26

CT FILE: Lee took over at Coventry from
ᴏʳmer Sunderland back-up goalkeeper
Murphy, debuting in August 2014 in the
ague Cup meeting with Cardiff City. He
ᴛ on to play 160 times for the Sky Blues,
of those appearances coming in the last
e seasons. He conceded four goals at the
ᴅium of Light for Coventry in April but
beaten just twice more in his remaining
four games.

CONOR McLAUGHLIN
DEFENDER

DATE SIGNED: 1ST JULY 2019
LAST CLUB: MILLWALL
**OTHER CLUBS: PRESTON NORTH END,
SHREWSBURY TOWN, FLEETWOOD TOWN**
INTERNATIONAL: NORTHERN IRELAND
AGE AT CHRISTMAS 2019: 28

FACT FILE: Conor is an experienced player who had 270 senior games to his name when he signed for Sunderland, exactly 200 of them for Fleetwood. No relation to goalkeeper Jon McLaughlin, Conor's debut had come in November 2010 in the Championship for Preston North End. The following season he joined Shrewsbury Town on loan before moving to Fleetwood who he helped to promotion in his second season when he was part of a defence that did not concede a goal in any of their three play-off games. Five days after that success, Conor made his international debut for Northern Ireland as a late sub against Uruguay, soon followed by a first start against Chile. At the time of his arrival on Wearside, Conor had 35 caps.

Impressive and consistent form led to a move to Millwall in the Championship in 2017 when he played in a 2-2 draw at the Stadium of Light for the Lions. Conor's brother, Ryan, plays for Rochdale and is also a Northern Ireland international.

THE ACADEMY OF LIGHT

NEW SIGNING 2019-20
JORDAN
WILLIS

JORDAN WILLIS
DEFENDER

DATE SIGNED: **13TH JULY 2019**
LAST CLUB: **COVENTRY CITY**
OTHER CLUBS: **NONE**
INTERNATIONAL: **ENGLAND UNDER 19**
AGE AT CHRISTMAS 2019: **25**

FACT FILE: Coventry born, Jordan played 208 times for his home town club, all but 14 of those games as starts. He is a speedy and determined defender who skippered the Sky Blues, with whom he won promotion from League Two in 2018 when he scored in the Wembley play-off final against Exeter. He was also a Wembley winner the previous season when he captained the Coventry team that beat Chris Maguire's Oxford in the Checkatrade Trophy final.

Willis was only 17 when he made his debut in a Championship fixture with Southampton on Guy Fawkes Day in 2011. He became a regular player two seasons later, playing in a 5-4 win over Bristol City – although he missed Coventry's freak 5-4 win at the Stadium of Light in 2019.

MICHAEL COLLINS
DEFENDER

DATE SIGNED: **4TH JULY 2019**
LAST CLUB: **EVERTON**
OTHER CLUBS: **NONE**
AGE AT CHRISTMAS 2019: **19**

FACT FILE: Michael had impressed with Wirral Boys before signing for Everton when he was 14. After four years with the Toffees, he left to come to Sunderland who he had been on trial with in April 2019. Michael actually managed to score for Sunderland in 2018, but in an Everton shirt as he deflected home a shot by Benji Kimpioka in an Under-18s match. His Under-18s debut for Everton came against Manchester United in August 2016. He went on to play 44 times at that level, scoring once. The first of two games for Everton at Under 23 level came against Derby in February 2018. Originally a left sided centre-back with Everton, he also operated extensively at left back for the Goodison Park club. Michael is eligible to play for the Republic of Ireland and Jamaica as well as England.

RUBEN SAMMUT
MIDFIELDER

DATE SIGNED: **4TH JULY 2019**
LAST CLUB: **CHELSEA**
OTHER CLUBS: **FALKIRK (LOAN)**
INTERNATIONAL: **SCOTLAND UNDER 21**
AGE AT CHRISTMAS 2019: **22**

FACT FILE: Ruben had played for Scotland up to Under 21 level before coming to Sunderland but the Maidstone born centre midfielder is still eligible to play for England and Malta. With Chelsea he was an unused sub as they defeated Fulham in the final of the FA Youth Cup in 2014 but he played in both legs of the 2015 and 2016 finals as Manchester City were beaten in both years. Those seasons also saw Sammut be part of the Blues team who won the UEFA Youth League, defeating Shakhtar Donetsk and PSG in the finals. In 2018/19, he obtained senior experience with 10 appearances on loan with Falkirk.

AHMED ABDELKADAR
GOALKEEPER

DATE SIGNED: **2ND JULY 2019**
LAST CLUB: **EU GUINGAMP**
OTHER CLUBS: **ENAD POLIS CHRYSOCHOUS (CYPRUS)**
AGE AT CHRISTMAS 2019: **20**

FACT FILE: This Algerian goalkeeper came to Sunderland from French club Guingamp. In 2018, he spent several weeks on loan to Leicester City where the Foxes then-manager Claude Puel decided not to sign the stopper who also has experience of playing in Cyprus.

NEW BOYS

LAURENS
DE BOCK
DEFENDER

DATE SIGNED: 2ND SEPTEMBER 2019
LAST CLUB: ON LOAN FROM LEEDS UNITED
OTHER CLUBS: HO KALKEN STANDARD WETTEREN, LOKEREN, CLUB BRUGGE, OOSTENDE (LOAN).
INTERNATIONAL: BELGIUM UNDER 21
AGE AT CHRISTMAS 2019: 27

FACT FILE: Laurens played two Champions League games against Manchester United for former European Cup finalists Club Brugge for whom he also 12 times in the Europa League, once scoring against HJK Helsinki. He won the Belgian League and Super Cup with Brugge in 2015 and the Belgian Cup in 2015 with Brugge and 2012 with Lokeren.

GEORGE
DOBSON
MIDFIELDER

DATE SIGNED: 25TH JULY 2019
LAST CLUB: WALSALL
OTHER CLUBS: ARSENAL, WEST HAM UNITED, SPARTA ROTTERDAM
AGE AT CHRISTMAS 2019: 22

FACT FILE: An energetic, tall, central midfielder who often captained his last club Walsall, Dobson gained youth experience with Arsenal and West Ham. He also gained experience of continental football with a spell in Netherlands with Sparta Rotterdam between July 2017 and January of the following year. In the top Dutch league, the Eredivisie, George played against VVV-Venlo, PEC Zwolle, NAC Breda, FC Twente and AZ Alkmaar.

Before going abroad, George had been on loan from West Ham to Walsall, first playing against Yeovil in August 2016. When he came back from the Netherlands, he was transferred to Walsall where he quickly became a regular member of the Saddlers' side. Last season, he made 44 appearances for Walsall, three of those coming against the Black Cats.

MARC McNULTY
STRIKER

DATE SIGNED: **24TH JULY 2019**
LAST CLUB: **ON LOAN FROM READING**
OTHER CLUBS: **LIVINGSTON, SHEFFIELD UNITED, PORTSMOUTH (LOAN), BRADFORD CITY (LOAN), COVENTRY CITY, HIBERNIAN (LOAN)**
INTERNATIONAL: **SCOTLAND**
AGE AT CHRISTMAS 2019: **27**

FACT FILE: On loan for a season from Reading, McNulty had 110 goals in 303 club games – including six hat-tricks – when he arrived at Sunderland. 28 of those came the season before last when he fired Coventry City to promotion into League One, that haul including two hat-tricks and two goals in the play-off semi-final before being Man of the Match at Wembley.

A natural goal-scorer, Marc marked his debut with a goal for Livingston in a victory at Montrose on Halloween 2009 and has maintained an excellent goals per game ratio. Last season he returned to Scotland on loan to Hibs from Reading and did so well he earned an international call up, making his Scotland debut in March.

JOEL LYNCH
DEFENDER

DATE SIGNED: **26TH AUGUST 2019**
LAST CLUB: **QPR**
OTHER CLUBS: **BRIGHTON, NOTTINGHAM FOREST, HUDDERSFIELD TOWN**
INTERNATIONAL: **WALES**
AGE AT CHRISTMAS 2019: **32**

FACT FILE: Joel joined Sunderland just before the transfer window closed. He is a Wales international who had spent the last ten years in the Championship before signing for Sunderland.

PLAYER PROFILES

*All statistics cover all competitions and are up to the start of the 2019-20 season

JON McLAUGHLIN
GOALKEEPER

SAFC APPEARANCES: **55**
SAFC CLEAN SHEETS: **15**
AGE AT CHRISTMAS 2019: **32**
SIGNED FROM: **HEART OF MIDLOTHIAN**
INTERNATIONAL: **SCOTLAND**

FACT FILE: Jon has been promoted with Bradford and Burton and has played in Wembley cup finals for Bradford and Sunderland.

TOM
FLANAGAN
DEFENDER

SAFC APPEARANCES: **42**
SAFC GOALS: **2**
AGE AT CHRISTMAS 2019: **28**
SIGNED FROM: **BURTON ALBION**
INTERNATIONAL: **NORTHERN IRELAND**

FACT FILE: Tom was once a team mate of former Sunderland winger John Oster at Barnet.

JAKE
HACKETT
MIDFIELDER

SAFC APPEARANCES: **3**
SAFC GOALS: **0**
AGE AT CHRISTMAS 2019: **19**
SIGNED FROM: **YOUTH PRODUCT**
INTERNATIONAL: **HAS BEEN SELECTED FOR ENGLAND YOUTH TRAINING SQUADS.**

FACT FILE: Jake made three appearances in the Checkatrade Trophy last season.

LUKE
O'NIEN
DEFENDER

SAFC APPEARANCES: **52**
SAFC GOALS: **5**
AGE AT CHRISTMAS 2019: **25**
SIGNED FROM: **WYCOMBE WANDERERS**

FACT FILE: Luke was born in England and is also eligible to play for Singapore.

JACK
BAINBRIDGE
DEFENDER

SAFC APPEARANCES: **2**
SAFC GOALS: **0**
AGE AT CHRISTMAS 2019: **21**
SIGNED FROM: **SWANSEA CITY**

FACT FILE: Jack started as a youth player with Everton.

JACK
BALDWIN
DEFENDER

SAFC APPEARANCES: **41**
SAFC GOALS: **3**
AGE AT CHRISTMAS 2019: **26**
SIGNED FROM: **PETERBOROUGH UNITED**

FACT FILE: Jack used to play for Hartlepool and is on a season long loan to Salford City.

40

ALIM
OZTURK
DEFENDER

SAFC APPEARANCES: **20**
SAFC GOALS: **0**
AGE AT CHRISTMAS 2019: **27**
SIGNED FROM: **BOLUSPOR**
INTERNATIONAL: **TURKEY UNDER 21**

FACT FILE: Ozturk is a former captain of Hearts.

DENVER
HUME
DEFENDER

SAFC APPEARANCES: **12**
SAFC GOALS: **0**
AGE AT CHRISTMAS 2019: **21**
SIGNED FROM: **YOUTH PRODUCT**

FACT FILE: As a boy, Denver played for the famous Cramlington Juniors team.

BRANDON
TAYLOR
DEFENDER

SAFC APPEARANCES: **1**
SAFC GOALS: **0**
AGE AT CHRISTMAS 2019: **20**
SIGNED FROM: **YOUTH PRODUCT**

FACT FILE: Brandon is a Sunderland supporter who has been with the club since he was 11.

MAX
POWER
MIDFIELDER

SAFC APPEARANCES: **46**
SAFC GOALS: **4**
AGE AT CHRISTMAS 2019: **26**
SIGNED FROM: **WIGAN ATHLETIC**

FACT FILE: Max won League One
with Wigan in 2018.

OWEN
GAMBLE
MIDFIELDER

SAFC APPEARANCES: **0**
SAFC GOALS: **0**
AGE AT CHRISTMAS 2019: **20**
SIGNED FROM: **DONCASTER ROVERS**

FACT FILE: Owen joined Sunderland
in 2015.

JORDAN
HUNTER
MIDFIELDER

SAFC APPEARANCES: **1**
SAFC GOALS: **0**
AGE AT CHRISTMAS 2019: **20**
SIGNED FROM: **LIVERPOOL**

FACT FILE: Jordan joined Sunderland on the same day as Dylan McGeouch.

GRANT
LEADBITTER
MIDFIELDER

SAFC APPEARANCES: **141**
SAFC GOALS: **11**
AGE AT CHRISTMAS 2019: **33**
SIGNED FROM: **MIDDLESBROUGH**
INTERNATIONAL: **ENGLAND UNDER 21**

FACT FILE: Grant is a former Middlesbrough Player of the Year and was named in the PFA Championship team of the year in 2015.

ELLIOTT
EMBLETON
MIDFIELDER

SAFC APPEARANCES: **4**
SAFC GOALS: **0**
AGE AT CHRISTMAS 2019: **20**
SIGNED FROM: **YOUTH PRODUCT**
INTERNATIONAL: **ENGLAND UNDER 20**

FACT FILE: Embleton won Grimsby's goal of the season last year for his strike against MK Dons in the FA Cup.

AIDEN
McGEADY
MIDFIELDER

SAFC APPEARANCES: **77**
SAFC GOALS: **21**
AGE AT CHRISTMAS 2019: **33**
SIGNED FROM: **EVERTON**
INTERNATIONAL: **REPUBLIC OF IRELAND**

FACT FILE: Aiden's dad, John, used to play for Sheffield United where he was a teammate of the great Celtic winger Jimmy Johnstone.

DAN
NEILL
MIDFIELDER

SAFC APPEARANCES: **1**
SAFC GOALS: **0**
AGE AT CHRISTMAS 2019: **18**
SIGNED FROM: **YOUTH PRODUCT**

FACT FILE: Dan debuted as an injury time sub in last season's Checkatrade Trophy game at Morecambe.

BALI **MUMBA**
MIDFIELDER

SAFC APPEARANCES: **9**
SAFC GOALS: **0**
AGE AT CHRISTMAS 2019: **18**
SIGNED FROM: **YOUTH PRODUCT**
INTERNATIONAL: **ENGLAND UNDER 18**

FACT FILE: When Bali made his debut, he became the fourth youngest player ever to play for Sunderland.

LYNDEN **GOOCH**
MIDFIELDER

SAFC APPEARANCES: **88**
SAFC GOALS: **9**
AGE AT CHRISTMAS 2019: **24**
(HIS BIRTHDAY IS ON CHRISTMAS EVE)
SIGNED FROM: **YOUTH PRODUCT**
INTERNATIONAL: **USA**

FACT FILE: One of Lynden's brothers is a professional surfer.

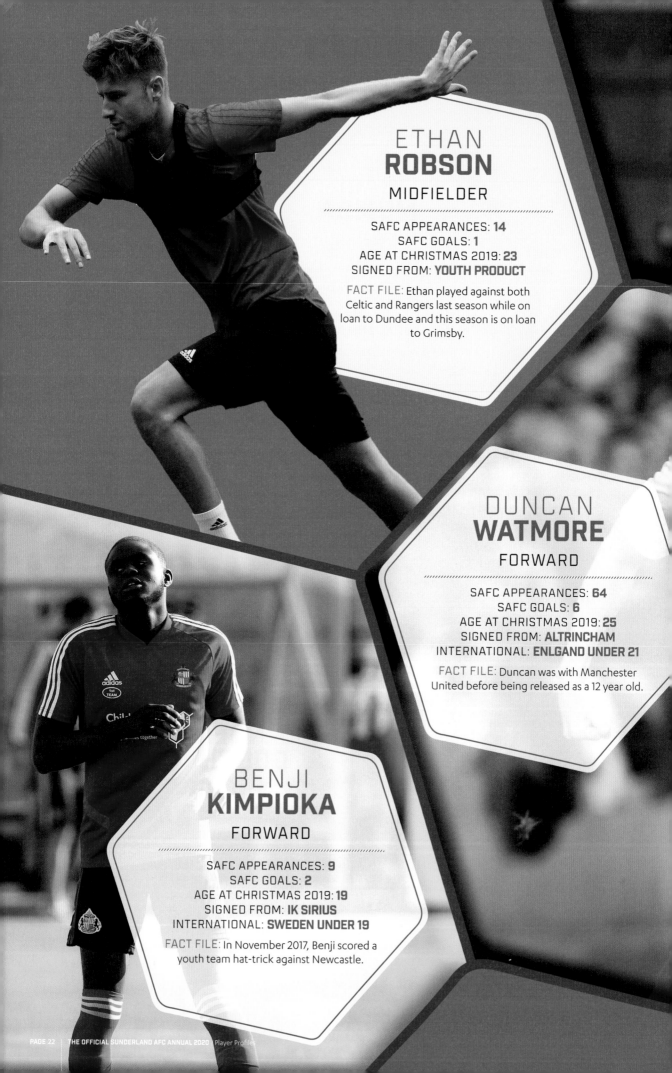

ETHAN
ROBSON
MIDFIELDER

SAFC APPEARANCES: **14**
SAFC GOALS: **1**
AGE AT CHRISTMAS 2019: **23**
SIGNED FROM: **YOUTH PRODUCT**

FACT FILE: Ethan played against both Celtic and Rangers last season while on loan to Dundee and this season is on loan to Grimsby.

DUNCAN
WATMORE
FORWARD

SAFC APPEARANCES: **64**
SAFC GOALS: **6**
AGE AT CHRISTMAS 2019: **25**
SIGNED FROM: **ALTRINCHAM**
INTERNATIONAL: **ENLGAND UNDER 21**

FACT FILE: Duncan was with Manchester United before being released as a 12 year old.

BENJI
KIMPIOKA
FORWARD

SAFC APPEARANCES: **9**
SAFC GOALS: **2**
AGE AT CHRISTMAS 2019: **19**
SIGNED FROM: **IK SIRIUS**
INTERNATIONAL: **SWEDEN UNDER 19**

FACT FILE: In November 2017, Benji scored a youth team hat-trick against Newcastle.

LEE CONNELLY
FORWARD

SAFC APPEARANCES: **2**
SAFC GOALS: **0**
AGE AT CHRISTMAS 2019: **20**
SIGNED FROM: **QUEEN'S PARK**
INTERNATIONAL: **SCOTLAND UNDER 17**

FACT FILE: Rangers and Burnley were keen to sign Lee when he joined Sunderland.

JACK DIAMOND
FORWARD

SAFC APPEARANCES: **3**
SAFC GOALS: **0**
AGE AT CHRISTMAS 2019: **19**
SIGNED FROM: **YOUTH PRODUCT**

FACT FILE: He joined Harrogate Town on loan from September 2019 to January 2020.

CHARLIE
WYKE
FORWARD

SAFC APPEARANCES: **30**
SAFC GOALS: **5**
AGE AT CHRISTMAS 2019: **27**
SIGNED FROM: **BRADFORD CITY**

FACT FILE: Last season's injury hit season was the first in four years where Wyke hadn't scored at least 15 goals.

CHRIS
MAGUIRE
MIDFIELDER

SAFC APPEARANCES: **43**
SAFC GOALS: **9**
AGE AT CHRISTMAS 2019: **30**
SIGNED FROM: **BURY**
INTERNATIONAL: **SCOTLAND**

FACT FILE: Chris has played for five other League One clubs: Portsmouth, Coventry, Rotherham, Oxford and Bury.

WILL
GRIGG
FORWARD

SAFC APPEARANCES: **21**
SAFC GOALS: **5**
AGE AT CHRISTMAS 2019: **28**
SIGNED FROM: **WIGAN ATHLETIC**
INTERNATIONAL: **NORTHERN IRELAND**

FACT FILE: Will scored twice as MK Dons beat Manchester United 4-0 in the League Cup, as well as scoring the winner when Wigan beat Manchester City 1-0 in the FA Cup in 2018.

JACK CONNOLLY
MIDFIELDER

SAFC APPEARANCES: **0**
SAFC GOALS: **0**
AGE AT CHRISTMAS 2019: **19**
SIGNED FROM: **ST. FRANCIS**
INTERNATIONAL: **REPUBLIC OF IRELAND
UNDER 16**

FACT FILE: Jack was with local Irish side St. Francis from the age of six to 16.

DYLAN McGEOUCH
MIDFIELDER

SAFC APPEARANCES: **30**
SAFC GOALS: **0**
AGE AT CHRISTMAS 2019: **26**
SIGNED FROM: **HIBERNIAN**
INTERNATIONAL: **SCOTLAND**

FACT FILE: During 2011-12 McGeouch's Celtic team mates included; Adam Matthews, Ki-Sung Yueng, Anthony Stokes and Glenn Loovens, all of whom have played for Sunderland.

SAMSON SHOWS YOU HOW TO MAKE...
EASY CUPCAKES

SAMSON COMES OVER ALL NIGELLA PAW-SON AND PROVIDES SUNDERLAND WITH SOME CUPS – WELL CUP-CAKES. IF THE TEAM WIN PROMOTION, THESE WOULD BE GREAT FOR A PROMOTION PARTY!

FOR THE CAKES YOU WILL NEED:

- **2** Large eggs
- **1** TEASPOON Vanilla essence
- **125**G Caster sugar
- **125**G Soft margarine
- **125**G Self-raising flour
- **100**G White ready to roll icing sugar
- **100**G Coloured fondant icing sugar including red and black

YOU WILL ALSO NEED:

- 12 paper cupcake cases
- A 12-hole bun baking tray
- Electric whisk if you have one or a wooden spoon
- Mixing bowl
- Rolling pin
- Small glass or jam jar lid
- Sharp knife (and a responsible adult for this part)

1. Wash your paws.

2. Pre-heat the oven to 180ºC / 350ºF / Gas mark 4.

3. Place the eggs, vanilla essence, sugar, margarine and flour in a mixing bowl and beat together with an electric mixer until the mixture is smooth and there are no lumps. This will take a few minutes. If you don't have a mixer you can use a wooden spoon but this will take a bit longer and is a bit harder to do. (You need to get an adult to help with this especially if you are using an electric mixer.)

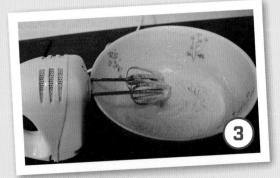

4 Carefully spoon the mixture evenly between the twelve cake cases.

5 Bake in the oven for approximately 15 – 20 minutes. The cakes will be ready when they have risen and are golden brown and will spring back when gently touched.

9 Place one on top of each cupcake.

10 Use the coloured icing and the sharp knife (with the help of a responsible adult) to cut shapes to decorate the top of the cakes. Here are some ideas for you to try.

6 Leave to cool for at least 30 minutes before decorating.

7 Roll out the white icing with the rolling pin until it is about 0.25cm thick.

8 Use the top of a glass or cup as a template and cut out twelve circles with a responsible adult helping you to use the sharp knife.

HAVE FUN SHARING THESE WITH YOUR FRIENDS.

HONOURING OUR LEGENDS
HALL OF FAME

THE SUNDERLAND HALL OF FAME CELEBRATES THE GREATEST NAMES IN THE HISTORY OF THE CLUB. THE FIRST 11 MEMBERS OF THIS HALL OF FAME WERE MADE MEMBERS AT A VERY SPECIAL OCCASION AT THE STADIUM OF LIGHT.

Players such as Niall Quinn, Jim Montgomery and Bobby Kerr were there to receive their awards. In the case of players from long ago who were being honoured, their children, grandchildren; or in the case of James Allan, his great-great-grandson were there to receive the awards in their names.

The intention is that every year, more players will be added to the Hall of Fame so that eventually all the people to have made a major impact at Sunderland will be honoured. This will include players from the women's game.

The first Hall of Fame dinner was hosted by Jeff Brown of the BBC with the awards handed out by SAFC director Charlie Methven. The first 11 members of the Hall of Fame were:

JAMES ALLAN

- James Allan was the man who started the club after introducing the sport of association football to Sunderland in 1879.

- As a player himself, he once scored an amazing 12 goals in one match! That is 12 just by James Allan. Sunderland won the match in 1884 by 23-0!

LEN ASHURST

- Record outfield appearance holder having played 458 games.
- Ever present in first ever promotion team in 1964.
- Managed the club.

CHARLIE BUCHAN

- Sunderland's all-time record league goal-scorer with 209 goals and 222 in total.
- Top scorer in 1912-13 title winning season when he also scored in the FA Cup semi-final as Sunderland reached the final for the first time.
- Along with Bobby Gurney, he is one of just two men to score five goals in a top-flight game for Sunderland.
- Played in England's first international at Wembley while with Sunderland.
- Later the publisher of the world's top selling football magazine 'Charles Buchan's Football Monthly' and the instigator of the Footballer of the Year Award.

JOHN AULD

- Scotland international John Auld was captain when Sunderland were league champions for the first time in 1892.
- He also played in the team when the league was won in 1893 and played a few games when 'The Team Of All The Talents' won the title again in 1895 – the same year Auld was part of the team when Sunderland became the world champions.
- After his playing days, John Auld helped Sunderland survive financially during the First World War.

SUNDERLAND AFC HALL OF FAME

HONOURING OUR LEGENDS
HALL OF FAME
INDUCTED 2019
RAICH CARTER

RAICH CARTER

- Captained Sunderland to their first ever FA Cup triumph, scoring the second goal in a 3-1 win over Preston in the 1937 final.
- Scored 31 goals as Sunderland won a sixth league title in 1935-36, when he skippered the team on the day the title was sealed.
- Famous England international who was world class in his day.

BOBBY GURNEY

- Top scorer in the club's history with 228 goals.
- Scored Sunderland's first ever goal at Wembley in helping to win the FA Cup in 1937.
- Scored 31 goals in 1935-36, including four on the day the league title was secured.
- Along with Buchan, one of just two players to score five times in one top-flight game for the Lads.
- England international.

CHARLIE HURLEY

- Voted Player of the Century in the Centenary Year of 1979.
- Captain of the first ever promotion team in 1964.
- Ever present that season when he was also runner up to Bobby Moore as Footballer of the Year.

BOBBY KERR

- Captain of the 1973 FA Cup winners.
- Sixth in the list of all time appearance makers.
- 1976 Division Two title winner.

NIALL QUINN

- Leading light in the record breaking 105-point promotion team of 1999.
- The scorer of the first goal and the first hat-trick at the Stadium of Light.
- The first man to score twice in a game at Wembley for Sunderland.
- Became manager and chairman as well as a tremendous player.

JIM MONTGOMERY

- Record appearance maker with a magnificent 627 games.
- Promotion winner in 1964 and 1976.
- Made the greatest save ever seen at Wembley in the 1973 FA Cup final to help Sunderland win the cup.

LEN SHACKLETON

- Renowned as 'The Clown Prince of Soccer.'
- The first of only three men to score 100 post-war goals for Sunderland.
- Perhaps the most popular player ever to represent the club.

BOARD GAME

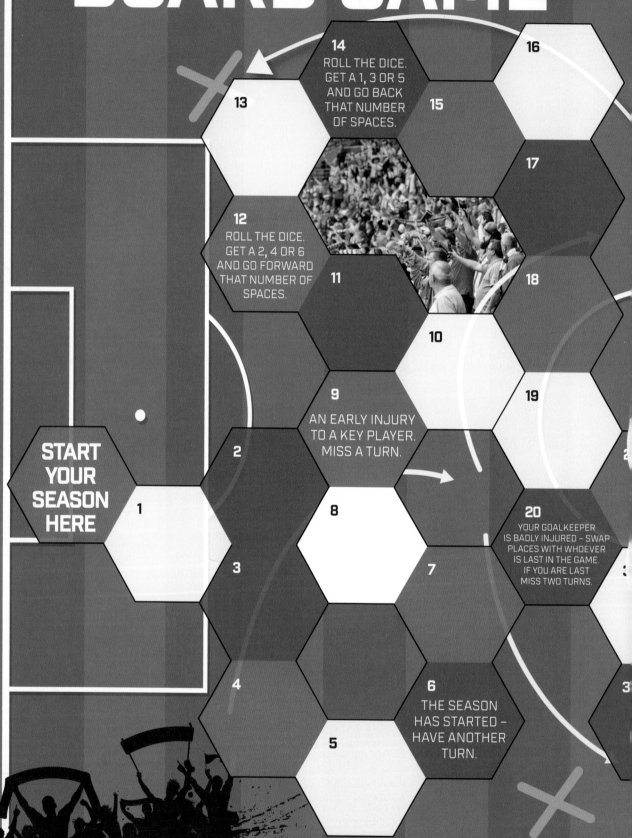

START YOUR SEASON HERE

1

2

3

4

5

6
THE SEASON HAS STARTED – HAVE ANOTHER TURN.

7

8

9
AN EARLY INJURY TO A KEY PLAYER. MISS A TURN.

10

11

12
ROLL THE DICE. GET A 2, 4 OR 6 AND GO FORWARD THAT NUMBER OF SPACES.

13

14
ROLL THE DICE. GET A 1, 3 OR 5 AND GO BACK THAT NUMBER OF SPACES.

15

16

17

18

19

20
YOUR GOALKEEPER IS BADLY INJURED – SWAP PLACES WITH WHOEVER IS LAST IN THE GAME. IF YOU ARE LAST MISS TWO TURNS.

28

27

29

26

30
BOOSTED BY A BIG JANUARY SIGNING. DOUBLE YOUR NEXT ROLL OF THE DICE.

24

25

31

23
YOU LOSE TWO GAMES IN A ROW – GO BACK TO 13.

32

46
FINAL GAME OF THE SEASON. ROLL THE DICE THREE TIMES. YOU NEED A TOTAL SCORE OF 10 OR MORE TO FINISH THE GAME.

22
ROLL THE DICE TWICE. IF YOUR TOTAL SCORE IS 10 OR MORE, SEND EVERY OTHER PLAYER BACK TO 1.

33
ALL YOUR RIVALS LOSE. GO FORWARD FOUR PLACES.

45

44

34

35

43
CRUCIAL LATE SEASON GAME. ROLL A 4, 5 OR 6 TO TAKE YOU PAST THE FINISHING POST. GET A 1, 2 OR 3 AND MOVE BACK THAT NUMBER OF SQUARES.

36
YOU MISS A LAST MINUTE PENALTY. MISS A TURN.

42

39
YOU HAVE TWO MEN SENT OFF. EVERY OTHER PLAYER MOVES FORWARD THREE PLACES.

41

40

GAME RULES

You'll need to find a dice and some counters, one counter for each person who wants to play.

Each player rolls the dice. Whoever gets the highest score goes first.

If two or more people have the same highest score, those people have another go each until someone wins.

Once you 'kick-off' after the first player's turn, it is the person on the left who goes second. Continue in that direction until you are back to the person who started.

Every player has to get a six before they can put their counter on the board, which they do by going straight to square six.

The winner is the first person to win promotion by passing square 46 first.

SEASON REVIEW

FOR THE FIRST TIME EVER, SUNDERLAND PLAYED AT WEMBLEY TWICE IN THE SAME SEASON. ON BOTH OCCASIONS THE LADS CAME SO CLOSE TO WINNING BUT TOUGH DISAPPOINTMENTS MEANT THAT THE BLACK CATS MISSED OUT BY THE NARROWEST OF MARGINS.

In the Checkatrade Trophy final against Portsmouth, the game finished 2-2 after extra time before Portsmouth won 5-4 in a penalty shoot-out. Portsmouth were played again in the play-offs, this time Sunderland winning 1-0 over two legs thanks to Chris Maguire's spectacular volley, but in the final at Wembley, a goal eight seconds from the end of injury time saw Charlton win promotion, leaving Sunderland to wonder what might have been.

Charlton had been the opponents on the first day of the season as well as the last. On that occasion, it was Sunderland's turn to win with a last minute winner, scored by Lynden Gooch. Starting and ending with the ecstasy and agony of those last minute goals Sunderland played 61 games – more than they ever had in one season and this is the story of a Sunderland revamped during the summer by new ownership, a new manager and a new look squad...

SUNDERLAND AFC V CHARLTON 4 AUG 2018

SUNDERLAND AFC V SCUNTHORPE 19 AUG 2018

SUNDERLAND AFC V ROCHDALE 22 SEPT 2018

SUNDERLAND AFC V BARNSLEY 27 NOV 2018

AUGUST TO NOVEMBER

August went very well with four wins and a draw away to eventual champions Luton. September wasn't so clever with just one win, a loss and three draws. However, after another draw – at home to Peterborough – at the beginning of October, Jack Ross' side won five league games in a row meaning they were second at the start of November. Despite a couple of draws, November ended with the game of the season, a superb 4-2 home win over Barnsley who would go on to claim the second automatic promotion place.

END OF MONTH POSITIONS

AUGUST	2ND	—o—
SEPTEMBER	4TH	↓
OCTOBER	3RD	↑
NOVEMBER	2ND	↑

By the end of November, the cups were well underway. Sheffield Wednesday had triumphed at the Stadium of Light in the Carabao Cup but all three Checkatrade Trophy games had been won (one on penalties) and FA Cup progress had been made at Port Vale.

SUNDERLAND AFC V SHEFFIELD WEDNESDAY 16 AUG 2018

SUNDERLAND AFC V BRADFORD
26 DECEMBER 2018

DECEMBER TO MARCH

Two wins, a draw and a loss kept Sunderland right in the promotion mix but without being able to gain the momentum needed to set the pace. Defeat at Portsmouth hinged on the sending off of Glenn Loovens who would not appear again all season. Despite that defeat at Fratton Park, the next game on Boxing Day smashed the previous League One attendance record when an incredible 46,039 saw a 1-0 win over Bradford City.

2019 began with a New Year's Day win at Blackpool but the remaining three games all brought draws, two of them against sides who went up, Charlton and Luton. Nonetheless, the run of draws left the Lads in third place as the last league game of the month was played.

The January transfer window saw Sunderland lose prolific young striker Josh Maja but invest a record League One fee of £3m for Will Grigg while also bringing midfielder Grant Leadbitter back to his boyhood club.

February began with a narrow win over AFC Wimbledon but this was frustratingly followed by a sequence of three more draws before Sunderland slipped into gear with three successive victories moving into March. A feisty draw at Wycombe was followed by yet another draw but this 0-0 at Barnsley was a good result at a promotion rival. Incredibly it was also the only league game all season in which Sunderland didn't score. Finally beating Walsall maintained third spot as attention turned to Wembley at the end of March.

END OF MONTH POSITIONS

DECEMBER	3RD	
JANUARY	3RD	—○—
FEBRUARY	3RD	—○—
MARCH	3RD	—○—

Walsall's previous visit to the SOL in December had ended FA Cup interest but the Checkatrade Trophy had seen Sunderland reach Wembley. Notts County had been knocked out, as had the Under 21 sides of Newcastle and Manchester City before a 2-0 semi-final win away to Bristol Rovers. A tournament record of 85,021 saw the final against Portsmouth where Aiden McGeady scored twice only for Sunderland to go down on penalties.

APRIL TO MAY

Despite being held to a home draw by Burton in the first home game after the cup final, Sunderland slipped into an automatic promotion place. This followed heartening back-to-back away wins at Accrington and Rochdale. No-one could have foreseen what happened next as in a freakish game, Sunderland conceded five times in a home league game for the first time since 1981 as Coventry won an amazing match 4-5. Although the team bounced back with a solid 2-0 home win over play-off bound Doncaster, it was to be the only victory in the final seven league games of the season; draws with Peterborough and Portsmouth preceding defeats at Fleetwood and Southend. The final place of fifth was to be Sunderland's lowest since the opening week of the season. For most of the year Sunderland had a game or more in hand so their regular position of third or fourth always looked as if it could be improved upon but ultimately Sunderland had to contend with the play-offs.

In the play-offs Sunderland did excellently to beat Portsmouth in the semi-final. Chris Maguire's volley proved enough to win the home leg where for the third time in the season, Sunderland lost a player (Alim Ozturk) to a red card that was later overturned. The second leg at Portsmouth saw a disciplined performance earn a goalless draw that took Sunderland to the final. At Wembley, there could not have been a better start as the Lads went a goal up early on through a spectacular own goal but Charlton levelled before half time and took the prize with Patrick Bauer's winner in the dying seconds.

It had been the longest of seasons, one full of incident with a team that fought all the way and played with spirit often married with style. In the final analysis they came up marginally short but it had been a season to remember and one in which once again the red and white army had excelled themselves.

END OF MONTH POSITIONS

APRIL	4TH	
MAY	5TH	

CHECKATRADE FINAL V PORTSMOUTH

SUNDERLAND AFC V DONCASTER 19 APRIL 2019

CHECKATRADE
TROPHY FINAL

OVER 40,000 SUNDERLAND FANS WERE IN THE PACKED WEMBLEY CROWD OF OVER 85,000 FOR THE 2019 CHECKATRADE TROPHY FINAL.

To reach the final Sunderland had to play seven games. They had only conceded one goal in the route to Wembley, in a 3-1 win over Carlisle United. Stoke City Under 21s (on penalties), Morecambe, Notts County and the Under 21 teams of Newcastle United and Manchester City had also been beaten before a semi-final away to Bristol Rovers. At Bristol, goals from Will Grigg and Lewis Morgan gave Sunderland a 2-0 victory and a passport to the final.

In the final against Portsmouth, Sunderland took a spectacular lead shortly before half-time when Aiden McGeady curled home a superb free-kick. Having led for 44 minutes, Jack Ross' team were pegged back eight minutes from the end when defender Nathan Thompson scored the first goal in his two years with the club.

The match went to extra-time and with just six minutes of that remaining, Jamal Lowe put Pompey ahead with a clever lob. Unlike in the play-off final back at Wembley a few weeks later, Sunderland had a chance to fight back and did so when McGeady got his second of the game with a minute to go.

Tied at 2-2 the match went to penalties. Aiden McGeady, Lynden Gooch, Max Power and Luke O'Nien all scored for Sunderland but Lee Cattermole's spot-kick was saved by Craig MacGillivray. With Portsmouth converting all five of their penalties they won the cup. It was tough on Sunderland who had fought hard and actually drawn the match.

#WONTBEHOMEFORTEA

TRAFALGAR SQUARE
TAKEOVER

THE RED AND WHITE ARMY PREPARE FOR WEMBLEY BY TAKING OVER TRAFALGAR SQUARE THE NIGHT BEFORE THE CHECKATRADE TROPHY FINAL. THERE WERE SIMILAR SCENES ON THE EVENING BEFORE THE PLAY-OFF FINAL A FEW WEEKS LATER.

1973 FA Cup winning midfielder Micky Horswill joined the fans in Trafalgar Square.

PLAY-OFF FINAL

THEY SAY LIGHTNING DOESN'T STRIKE TWICE – BUT IT DOES FOR SUNDERLAND AT WEMBLEY.

56 days earlier The Lads had lost the Checkatrade Trophy final on penalties. This time the Red and White army suffered the blow of losing to a goal eight seconds from the end of extra-time. Those were the only eight seconds in the game that Sunderland were behind.

Sunderland had gone ahead after just five minutes to a freak own goal when Charlton 'keeper Dillon Phillips took his eye off the ball and allowed a back-pass from Naby Sarr to go under his foot and into the net. It was the 12th goal Sunderland have ever scored at Wembley - and none of them were from as far out as this O.G.!

Sunderland led for half an hour before Ben Purrington upset the Black Cats by clawing Charlton back into the game with his first goal since joining the club on loan from Rotherham. After almost a further hour's play, the game looked set for extra-time when Charlton were given a free-kick wide on the left. Defender Patrick Bauer got two bites at the cherry, his first effort being blocked but the second seeing the German defender scramble the ball home for his only goal of the season.

There was no time for Sunderland to come back. As in their previous Wembley meeting when Charlton beat Sunderland on penalties in the 1998 Championship play-off, the tiniest fraction resulted in the Londoners experiencing ecstasy while the Wearsiders trudged the length of the country home disappointed but determined to come back stronger.

After losing to Charlton in the play-off final at the old Wembley, Sunderland bounced back to win the league with a record number of points the following season. Responding by winning automatic promotion following play-off defeat is now the ambition once again.

#NOTDONEYET

JON
MCLAUGHLIN
PLAYER OF THE YEAR

Since selling not only Jordan Pickford but also Vito Mannone when they dropped out of the Premier League, Sunderland had struggled badly in a position where traditionally they are strong – goalkeeper.

Thankfully **Jon McLaughlin** arrived in the summer of 2018 to take over as Sunderland's number one. The Scotland international was excellent all season. Consistency is the key thing for goalkeepers and McLaughlin could be counted upon every week to not only not let the team down, but time after time make key saves to help earn vital results.

Ever present in the league, the Scotland international played a total of 55 times in all competitions, his composure and authority always giving confidence to the defenders in front of him as they knew exactly what to expect of their 'keeper.

While McLaughlin lifted the club's official Player of the Year award, winger **Aiden McGeady** scooped the Supporters' Association Player of the Season accolade. Like McLaughlin, McGeady was a worthy winner. The Irish international's natural ability never in doubt but supporters also saw the veteran

giving it his all in every game. Towards the end of the season, he regularly played when in pain and needing special treatment to get him on the pitch – but Sunderland were still a better team with him than without him.

Below: Aiden McGeady won the Supporters' Association Player of the Year award

Luke O'Nien was the convinc[ing]
Sunderland's Young Player of th[e]

ROCKIN' ALL OVER LEAGUE ONE

Luke O'Nien was the convincing winner of Sunderland's Young Player of the Year award in his first season at the club. A promotion winner with Wycombe Wanderers in the season before coming to Wearside, O'Nien started slowly at Sunderland, often being substitute in his early weeks.

His energy and determination in midfield endeared him to the crowd, as did the steadily growing list of stories of the player going out of his way to be approachable and show how much he wanted to be part of things at Sunderland.

Eventually tried at right back, O'Nien made the position his own. His ability to motor up and down the flank made Luke a natural for the position. Despite the defensive position he continued to be a threat going forward, scoring, claiming assists and winning penalties.

Just 23 at the start of the season, in total O'Nien appeared in 52 games in his first season, scoring five goals.

Signed from Wycombe Wanderers for whom he played 119 times, O'Nien started with Watford, making one appearance for them in the Championship back in March 2014 , the month Sunderland met Manchester City at Wembley in the League (Capital One) Cup final.

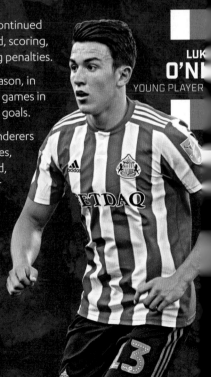

LUK[E]
O'N[IEN]
YOUNG PLAYER

TEST YOURSELF ON 2019

HOW MUCH NOTICE HAVE YOU TAKEN OF 2019?
TAKE THE TEST ON THE YEAR JUST GONE AND
SEE HOW WELL YOU CAN DO.

01 WHO DID SUNDERLAND PLAY
ON NEW YEAR'S DAY 2019?

07 HOW MANY DIFFERENT SCORERS (IN Q6)
WERE THERE IN THAT GAME: 3. 6 OR 9?

02 WHO DID SUNDERLAND SIGN FROM
MIDDLESBROUGH IN JANUARY?

08 WHO DID SUNDERLAND SIGN
WILL GRIGG FROM?

03 KAZAIAH STERLING JOINED ON LOAN IN JANUARY
FROM WHICH PREMIER LEAGUE LONDON CLUB?

04 WHO WERE SUNDERLAND PLAYING IN THE ONLY ONE OF THEIR 46
LEAGUE GAMES THAT THEY DID NOT SCORE IN DURING 2018-19?

05 WHO DID SUNDERLAND BEAT IN THE SEMI-FINAL
OF THE CHECKATRADE TROPHY FINAL?

06 WHO WERE SUNDERLAND
PLAYING WHEN THEY LOST 4-5 IN APRIL?

09 WHO DID SUNDERLAND DEFEAT IN THE PLAY-OFF SEMI-FINALS?

NABY SARR OWN GOAL

10 WHO SCORED THE ONLY GOAL OF THE PLAY-OFF SEMI-FINAL?

11 CHARLTON'S NABY SARR SCORED AN OWN GOAL FOR SAFC IN THE PLAY-OFF FINAL – WHAT NATIONALITY IS HE?

12 DID THE CHECKATRADE TROPHY FINAL OR THE LEAGUE ONE PLAY OFF FINAL HAVE THE HIGHEST ATTENDANCE?

OR

13 WHO WAS THE PLAYER ON LOAN FROM BURNLEY EARLY IN 2019?

14 WHO WAS THE WINGER BORROWED FROM CELTIC IN THE FIRST HALF OF 2019?

15 WHO WAS SUNDERLAND'S PLAYER OF THE SEASON FOR 2018-19?

16 WHO WAS SUNDERLAND'S YOUNG PLAYER OF THE SEASON FOR 2018-19?

17 WHO DID REECE JAMES LEAVE SUNDERLAND FOR DURING THE SUMMER?

FIND THE ANSWERS ON PAGE 61

HOW WELL DID YOU DO?

18-20	CHAMPIONS
16-17	RUNNERS' UP
14-15	PLAY-OFF WINNERS
13	PLAY-OFF RUNNERS' UP
11-12	PLAY-OFF SEMI-FINALISTS
8-10	TOP HALF
6-7	BOTTOM HALF BUT SAFE
3-5	JUST ESCAPED RELEGATION
1-2	RELEGATED
0	BOTTOM OF THE TABLE

18 WHO STARRED AT THE STADIUM OF LIGHT IN THE SUMMER POP CONCERT?

19 WHO WAS SUNDERLAND'S FIRST GAME OF 2019-20 AGAINST?

20 WHO DID SUNDERLAND FACE IN THEIR FIRST CUP-TIE OF 2019-20?

SUNDERLAND'S SCOTS

RIGHT FROM THE VERY START OF THE CLUB'S HISTORY IN 1879, SCOTTISH PLAYERS HAVE BEEN A VITAL PART OF SUNDERLAND. THE PERSON WHO BROUGHT FOOTBALL TO SUNDERLAND AND STARTED THE CLUB WAS JAMES ALLAN, A SCHOOL TEACHER FROM AYRSHIRE. HERE WE REMEMBER SOME OF THE IMPORTANT SCOTTISH PLAYERS TO HAVE PLAYED THEIR PART AT SUNDERLAND.

JIM BAXTER

WHEN DID HE PLAY?
1965-67

WHAT POSITION WAS HE?
MIDFIELD

NUMBER OF CAPS?
34

WHY WAS HE SO GOOD?
Baxter was one of the most skilful players to ever represent Sunderland. His ability to control a ball and pass with precision was legendary. His left foot was known as 'the claw'. He would tell young forwards to just run to where they thought they wanted the ball and when they got there the ball would be arriving for them – and he could make sure it was. Chosen for a 'Rest of the World' team against England in 1963, when Scotland beat World Champions England at Wembley in 1967 Baxter was the star man, while he was on Sunderland's books.

CHARLIE THOMPSON

WHEN DID HE PLAY?
1908-15

WHAT POSITION WAS HE?
DEFENDER

NUMBER OF CAPS?
21

WHY WAS HE SO GOOD?
Charlie Thompson was already quite an old and experienced player when he moved to England to join Sunderland. He was a really tough centre-half. Football was very different when Charlie played compared to how it is now. It was a much rougher game and Thompson could physically stand up to the hardest opponents. He was a major influence in Sunderland becoming league champions in the same season they reached their first ever FA Cup final in 1913.

CRAIG GORDON

WHEN DID HE PLAY?
2007-12

WHAT POSITION WAS HE?
GOALKEEPER

NUMBER OF CAPS?
54 SO FAR

WHY WAS HE SO GOOD?
When Roy Keane signed Craig Gordon he made him the most expensive goalkeeper in British football. The fee of £9m was huge. Gordon was so good that his save from Bolton's Zat Knight was officially rated the best save in the first 20 years of the Premier League. An agile and athletic goalkeeper, his strength was his ability to make spectacular saves. Craig unluckily suffered from serious injury problems but came back to star for Celtic.

GEORGE MULHALL

WHEN DID HE PLAY?
1962-69

WHAT POSITION WAS HE?
WINGER

NUMBER OF CAPS?
3

WHY WAS HE SO GOOD?
Mulhall was tough. He was fast. He was direct. He was brave. He scored goals as well as making them and he linked up with his teammates. He played every game when Sunderland won promotion in 1964 and he was excellent in the top flight. One of his Scotland caps is on display at the Stadium of Light and one of his international shirts can be seen at the Academy.

ALLAN JOHNSTON

WHEN DID HE PLAY?
1997-99

WHAT POSITION WAS HE?
WINGER

NUMBER OF CAPS?
18

WHY WAS HE SO GOOD?
Known as 'Magic' Johnston, Allan was on the wing when Sunderland got a record 105 points when winning promotion to the Premier League in 1999. Right-footed, he played on the left. He would cut inside and score with spectacular shots or link up with overlapping left back Michael Gray. The pair were brilliant together. Some wingers like to beat their man and get a cross in – as George Mulhall did. Johnston was more of what is known as a jinky winger. He wasn't fast but he had the skill to beat a defender, and then beat him again if he had to.

JON MCLAUGHLIN

WHEN DID HE PLAY?
2018-PRESENT

WHAT POSITION WAS HE?
GOALKEEPER

NUMBER OF CAPS?
1 SO FAR

WHY WAS HE SO GOOD?
Jon McLaughlin solved Sunderland's problem in goal. In the year before he arrived in 2018 Sunderland had struggled in a position which has traditionally been a strength at the club. McLaughlin became very popular by making a lot of excellent saves and most importantly by being consistent and reliable. He even became the first ever Sunderland goalie to save a penalty at the Stadium of Light.

HAPPY CHRISTMAS

THIS CHRISTMAS HOPEFULLY YOU AND YOUR FAMILY WILL HAVE LOTS OF CHRISTMAS CARDS. DID YOU KNOW THAT EVERY YEAR SUNDERLAND AFC PRODUCES ITS OWN CHRISTMAS CARDS? MAYBE ONE DAY YOU WILL RECEIVE ONE!

Take a look at the selection of SAFC Christmas cards here. Some of these cards show Sunderland's old ground Roker Park and some have the old club badge featuring a ship. More modern cards often show the Stadium of Light and the modern badge. Which of these cards do like the best and which one do you like the least?

When you look at your own Christmas cards, how many have Santa Claus on them? Notice he's wearing Sunderland colours!

SUNDERLAND ASSOCIATION FOOTBALL CLUB

HAVE A PURRR... FECT CHRISTMAS FROM ALL AT SUNDERLAND AFC

Christmas Past...   *...Christmas Present...*   *...and Christmas Future*

Seasons Greetings from Sunderland A.F.C.   *Your Caring Club*

SEASONS GREETINGS

WHAT SUNDERLAND WORE

STYLES CHANGE BUT THE RED AND WHITE STRIPES REMAIN. ALTHOUGH SUNDERLAND'S FIRST EVER KIT WAS ACTUALLY BLUE AND WHEN THEY FIRST SWITCHED TO RED AND WHITE IT WAS RED AND WHITE HALVES (LIKE BLACKBURN BUT RED AND WHITE). THE RED AND WHITE STRIPES HAVE BEEN PART OF SUNDERLAND'S STRIP SINCE BEFORE OUR GRANDPARENTS WERE BORN. TAKE A LOOK AT THESE SUNDERLAND KITS THROUGH THE AGES AND SEE WHICH ONE YOU LIKE THE BEST.

1971-72
DICK MALONE

1950s
DON REVIE

1960s
NEIL MARTIN

1919-20
BARNEY TRAVERS

1901-02
BILLY HOGG

1930s
RAICH CARTER

1912-13
ARTHUR BRIDGETT

1989-90
THOMAS HAUSER

1997-98
ANDY MELVILLE

1985-86
ERIC GATES

1987-88
JOHN CORNFORTH

1981-82
ALLY MCCOIST

1983-84
PAUL ATKINSON

1980-81
SAM ALLARDYCE

1980s

2008-09
GEORGE MCCARTNEY

1999-00
CHRIS MAKIN

AND A LOOK AT SOME 'LOVELY'
EIGHTIES TRACKSUITS MODELLED BY
PETER DAVENPORT. MARCO GABBIADINI.
GARY BENNETT AND TONY NORMAN
WITH ASSISTANT MANAGER VIV BUSBY
AT THE FRONT.

DESIGN A KIT

You've seen Sunderland's modern kits and have viewed some of Sunderland's old strips on the previous pages. Can you come up with a better kit for the Lads? Colour in the picture here and come up with your idea of the best ever Sunderland kit.

PUZZLE IT OUT

SPOT THE SCORELINE

SUNDERLAND SCORED FOUR GOALS IN FIVE LEAGUE ONE MATCHES LAST SEASON. CAN YOU MATCH THE GAME TO THE SCORELINE? For instance, if you think Sunderland won 4-2 against Rochdale then write 4-2 next to number 3. The five scorelines were all either 4-1, 4-2 or 4-5.

1 SUNDERLAND V COVENTRY CITY

2 SUNDERLAND V BARNSLEY

3 SUNDERLAND V ROCHDALE

4 GILLINGHAM V SUNDERLAND

5 SUNDERLAND V GILLINGHAM

CREST TEST

All of these badges above are from clubs in the same division as Sunderland. Can you name them?

1

2

3

4

5

EYE-DENTIFY

Can you spot the player just from his eyes?

1

2

3

4

FIND THE ANSWERS ON PAGE 61.

PUZZLE IT OUT

SPOT THE DIFFERENCE

CAN YOU SPOT THE EIGHT DIFFERENCES IN THE ACTION SHOTS BELOW?

FIND THE ANSWERS ON PAGE 61.

SAMSON'S SUMS

USE THE SUNDERLAND SQUAD NUMBERS TO HELP SAMSON DO HIS SUMS. FOR INSTANCE THE ANSWER TO QUESTION ONE IS 16 BECAUSE MAX POWER IS NUMBER 6 AND MARC MCNULTY IS NUMBER 10.

1 MAX POWER + MARC MCNULTY =

2 JORDAN WILLIS + LYNDEN GOOCH =

3 CHRIS MAGUIRE + DUNCAN WATMORE =

4 ALIM OZTURK + CHARLIE WYKE =

5 WILL GRIGG + DENVER HUME =

6 GRANT LEADBITTER − LUKE O'NIEN =

7 AIDEN MCGEADY − TOM FLANAGAN =

8 GEORGE DOBSON − JACK BALDWIN =

9 CONOR MCLAUGHLIN × DYLAN MCGEOUCH =

10 GLENN LOOVENS ÷ MAX POWER =

2019/20 SQUAD NUMBERS

1	JON MCLAUGHLIN	**11**	LYNDEN GOOCH	**21**	ETHAN ROBSON
2	CONOR MCLAUGHLIN	**12**	TOM FLANAGAN	**22**	WILL GRIGG
4	JORDAN WILLIS	**13**	LUKE O'NIEN	**23**	GRANT LEADBITTER
5	ALIM OZTURK	**14**	DUNCAN WATMORE	**24**	GLENN LOOVENS
6	MAX POWER	**15**	JACK BALDWIN	**31**	BENJI KIMPIOKA
7	CHRIS MAGUIRE	**16**	LEE BURGE	**33**	DENVER HUME
8	DYLAN MCGEOUCH	**17**	ELLIOT EMBLETON	**43**	ANTHONY PATTERSON
9	CHARLIE WYKE	**18**	GEORGE DOBSON		
10	MARC MCNULTY	**19**	AIDEN MCGEADY		

FIND THE ANSWERS ON PAGE 61.

GOT, NOT GOT.

HAVE YOU EVER COLLECTED FOOTBALL STICKERS OR CARDS? TAKE A LOOK AT SOME OF THESE SUNDERLAND STICKERS AND CARDS FROM YEARS GONE BY.

How many have you heard of? You might have to ask older members of the family to tell you what they remember about some of these players.

Ask your mam or dad if they collected stickers or cards and if they still have any they can show you.

Stickers and cards are always great to look back on but of course they can be frustrating when you are trying to complete the set and keep getting the same sticker!

RAICH CARTER
Midfielder

CHARLIE HURLEY
Centre Half

CLAUDIO REYNA
Midfielder

MARCO GABBIADINI
Striker

BERNT HAAS
Defender

BOB STOKOE
Manager

STAN ANDERSON
Midfielder

MICHAEL GRAY
Midfielder

JIM MONTGOMERY
Goalkeeper

KEVIN BALL
Defender/Midfielder

GARY BENNETT
Defender

JIM BAXTER
Midfielder

ALEX RAE
Midfielder

BOBBY KERR
Midfielder

KEVIN PHILLIPS
Striker

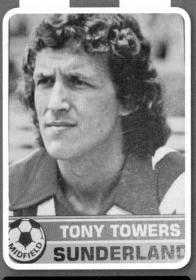

TONY TOWERS
Midfielder

FOUNDATION OF LIGHT

BEACON OF LIGHT

NEXT TO THE STADIUM OF LIGHT YOU WILL SEE THE BEACON OF LIGHT, HOME OF SUNDERLAND AFC CHARITY FOUNDATION OF LIGHT. OPEN FOR EVERYONE SEVEN DAYS A WEEK, INSIDE THE BEACON ARE EDUCATION, HEALTH & WELLBEING, AND WORLD OF WORK ZONES. IT HAS 5-A-SIDE PITCHES, A SEVEN-A-SIDE ROOFTOP PITCH, HUGE INDOOR SPORTS ARENA AND MUCH MORE, AND REGULARLY HOSTS SPORTS EVENTS AND THE FOUNDATION'S FOOTBALL COACHING PROGRAMMES.

VISIT **BEACONOFLIGHT.CO.UK**

QUIZ AND PUZZLE
ANSWERS

PAGES 46–47: TEST YOURSELF ON 2019

1. BLACKPOOL
2. GRANT LEADBITTER
3. TOTTENHAM HOTSPUR
4. BARNSLEY
5. BRISTOL ROVERS
6. COVENTRY
7. 9
8. WIGAN
9. PORTSMOUTH
10. CHRIS MAGUIRE
11. FRENCH
12. CHECKATRADE TROPHY FINAL
13. JIMMY DUNNE
14. LEWIS MORGAN
15. JON MCLAUGHLIN
16. LUKE O'NIEN
17. DONCASTER ROVERS
18. THE SPICE GIRLS
19. OXFORD UNITED
20. ACCRINGTON STANLEY

PAGE 55: SPOT THE SCORELINE

1. **4-5** 2. **4-2** 3. **4-1** 4. **1-4** 5. **4-2**

PAGE 55: EYE-DENTIFY

1. **GEORGE DOBSON**   2. **WILL GRIGG**   3. **LEE BURGE**   4. **ALIM OZTURK**

PAGE 55: CREST TEST

 BURTON ALBION

 SUNDERLAND AFC

 BOLTON WANDERERS

 **IPSWICH TOWN**

 BRISTOL ROVERS

PAGE 56: SPOT THE DIFFERENCE

PAGE 57: SAMSON'S SUMS

1. **16**   2. **15**   3. **21**   4. **14**   5. **55**
6. **10**   7. **7**   8. **3**   9. **16**   10. **4**